CATALINA ISLAND TRAVEL GUIDE

Catalina Island Uncovered: Your Insider's Guide to Paradise, The Premier Traveler's Handbook, Must-see Sights, Essential Travel Guide, and Passport to Island Wonders

D1707428

Michael M. Brown

Table of Contents

My Vacation Story in Catalina Island

I can still feel the excitement I felt as I looked out the ferry window and enjoyed the fresh ocean breeze on my face. A gem right off the coast of California called Catalina Island awaiting my arrival. I had been looking forward to this vacation trip for weeks, and now, after much anticipation, I was ready to go on it.

I couldn't help but reflect on how I had always desired to be away from the rush of city life as the ferry sailed over the calm waters. I experienced an immediate sense of calm as soon as I arrived on the island. I was able to completely unwind and take in the grandeur of this natural wonder since it seemed as though time had stopped.

The breathtaking natural beauty of Catalina Island was the first thing that caught my attention. I was in amazement with the rocky coastline, verdant mountains, and immaculate beaches. Despite having seen innumerable images of the island, nothing could have prepared me for the reality. It was a beautiful paradise, and I was determined to see everything there was to see.

My first day was spent wandering around the quaint village of Avalon. Boutique stores and beautiful houses adorned the quiet streets. I couldn't help but feel compelled to try some of the local restaurant's fresh fish. Every bite had an ocean flavor, which gave me the impression that I was actually on vacation. I strolled along Crescent Avenue, pausing to take in the old Catalina Casino, a monument to the island's illustrious past.

My explorations continued with a trip to the Catalina Island Museum, where I discovered the island's intriguing past and how it went from being a secluded refuge to a well-liked vacation spot. The legends of famous tourists and

Hollywood celebrities that frequented the island in the past gave my trip an intriguing dimension.

When I made the decision to tour the island's interior, it was one of the most memorable parts of my trip. I took a trip through the lush vegetation and fauna of the Catalina Island Conservancy. The air was thick with the aroma of eucalyptus trees, and I was accompanied on my travels by the songs of local birds. I also came upon a herd of bison that had been left behind from a 1920s movie set and were now living on the island. Getting a close-up look at these majestic animals was a strange experience.

I couldn't help but want to jump into the seas surrounding the island, which were incredibly clear. Snorkelers will find Catalina Island to be a haven, therefore I wasn't going to pass up the chance to discover the fascinating underwater world. I was met by a rainbow of marine life when I dove beneath the surface of the water. I had the impression of entering another world as a result of the vibrant fish and flowing kelp forests. I started snorkeling every day because I couldn't get enough of the stunning underwater scenery.

I also visited the renowned Two Harbors, a remote haven on the island's west end, while I was there. We cruised by sea caves and craggy rocks on our voyage, which in and of itself was an adventure. A modest harbor and a laid-back vibe might be found in Two Harbors, a tranquil haven. I had a wonderful seafood lunch at Harbor Reef and then had a leisurely stroll along the beach to take in the area's natural beauty.

It goes without saying that no trip to Catalina Island would be complete without taking part in its exhilarating excursions. I made the decision to go ziplining, and the experience was really thrilling. I experienced an adrenaline rush as I flew above the island's canyons and valleys while admiring the mesmerizing panoramic vistas. It was an adventure that stretched my capabilities and gave me a sense of satisfaction.

I relished the breathtaking sunsets on the island as the sun went below the horizon. Every evening, I chose a different location to observe the sky turn into a work of art filled with vivid oranges and purples. These moments served as a reminder of Catalina Island's natural beauty and tranquility.

A glass-bottom boat cruise was among my trip's most memorable activities. I was able to experience the undersea world without getting wet thanks to it. The boat's transparent bottom revealed an array of fascinating marine life, including kelp forests, colorful fish, and even a glimpse of a joyful sea lion. It was a fascinating and instructive experience that deepened my awareness of the island's aquatic ecosystem.

I had a fun outdoor performance at Wrigley Stage on my final night on Catalina Island. The live music, played beneath a sky filled with stars, was the ideal way to end my fantastic trip. I danced, laughed, made new friends, and felt really thankful for the amazing experience I had had the previous week.

I felt mixed emotions as I left Catalina Island. I had become quite close to this lovely area, and it had made a deep impression on my soul. My heart would always hold the memories of this vacation excursion on Catalina Island. I was aware that I would carry the island's beauty and peace with me as I rode the ferry back to the mainland, serving as a constant reminder to pull back from the hustle and bustle of daily life and appreciate the quiet of nature. It had truly been a paradise on Catalina Island, and I will always be appreciative.

Introduction

Greetings from Catalina Island

Welcome to Catalina Island, a magical Pacific island located just off the coast of Southern California. Catalina Island is a destination for tourists looking for a singular getaway from the rush and bustle of everyday life because of its pristine waters, untamed landscapes, and Mediterranean charm.

The island is a fascinating location for cultural discovery because of its rich history, which starts with its Native American roots. There is something for everyone among its many activities, which range from trekking along picturesque routes to snorkeling in pristine bays.

Whether you're planning a family trip, a solitary adventure, or a romantic break, Catalina Island is certain to leave you with priceless memories. We'll reveal the mysteries of this secluded paradise in this book and offer advice on how to get the most out of your time there.

Concerning This Travel Guide

Your ticket to a memorable Catalina Island experience is our travel guide. We want to be your expert guide while you're here, providing insightful advice that will enable you to get the most out of your stay. We cover everything, from useful information to must-see sights.

We recognize that each tourist is unique, which is why this guide is made to accommodate a wide variety of interests. We've compiled material to make sure you have an outstanding experience on Catalina Island, whether you're an outdoor enthusiast, a history buff, or just want to unwind by the beach.

So, as you set off to explore this island paradise, think of this guide as your reliable companion, ready to provide you all the information you require to make your trip genuinely memorable.

How to reach Catalina Island

The first thrilling stage of your island experience is getting to Catalina Island. From several locations along the Southern California coastline, it is easy to reach this gorgeous location. The most popular method of getting to the island is by ferry, which leaves from towns including Long Beach, Dana Point, and San Pedro on the mainland.

A helicopter flight that provides amazing aerial views of the island is an option if you're seeking for a more breathtaking welcome. The trip to Catalina Island is sure to be a highlight of your whole visit, whether you take the ferry or the helicopter.

It's crucial to organize your vacation based on your location and preferences before we get into the intricacies of transportation. Let's look at how to go to this lovely island.

Ideal Season to Visit

Your experience on Catalina Island will be greatly influenced by the time of year you visit. Although the island's Mediterranean environment guarantees moderate weather all year round, certain seasons provide particular benefits.

A popular season is spring, which lasts from April to June. The island blossoms with wildflowers at this season, and it's pleasantly warm outside. For outdoor pursuits like hiking and snorkeling, the time is ideal.

The busiest travel season is throughout the summer, from June to August. Be prepared for warmer weather as well as crowded beaches and attractions. This might be the best time to visit if you like vibrant settings and water sports.

The fall season, which lasts from September through November, is milder and less crowded. It's a great option for a peaceful getaway and a more laid-back experience.

The least active time of year is the winter, from December to March. The cooler months are ideal for isolation, cozy vacations, and taking in the tranquil charm of the island.

When organizing your trip to Catalina Island, take into account your tastes and hobbies. Every season has its own distinct attraction, giving a fantastic experience all year long.

Essential Travel Advice

It's critical to be organized if you want to enjoy your Catalina Island experience to the fullest. Following are some crucial pointers to improve your experience:
Pack wisely: Bring cozy clothing, walking shoes, and extra layers for chilly evenings if you're coming in spring or fall.

Reserved Space Matters: Especially during the busy season, reserve your lodging, boat or helicopter flights, and activities in advance.
Island Money: Despite the fact that the U.S. dollar is accepted, it's a good idea to carry some

cash just in case, as some locations might prefer it.

Transportation: Make a reservation for the ferry in advance if you intend to bring your car. Alternatively, you can walk around the island or rent a golf cart to go around.

Dining Options: The island offers a variety of luxury to informal dining options. Enjoy some fresh seafood and learn about the regional cuisine.

Outdoor adventurers will find Catalina to be a refuge. For water sports, remember to include sunscreen, caps, and swimwear. Don't forget your comfortable shoes when hiking.

Respect the environment: Catalina is renowned for its beautiful setting. Respect the Leave No Trace guidelines to assist with preserving our stunning island.

By paying attention to these suggestions, you'll be ready to visit Catalina Island with ease and enjoy yourself to the fullest.

Investigating the Island

Discover the natural splendor and one-of-a-kind attractions that Catalina Island has to offer. You won't want to miss these highlights, to name a few:

Avalon: The capital of the island, Avalon, is a gorgeous coastal town with quaint lanes, shops, and delectable restaurants. Enjoy Crescent Avenue's architecture, which is influenced by the Mediterranean.

Descanso Beach: Descanso Beach is a great place to unwind on a sunny day. You can swim in the pristine waters there or relax with a drink at the beachfront bar.

Catalina Casino: Despite its name, this ancient structure is not a place of gambling. It is a famous building with a theater, a ballroom, and stunning views from the rooftop.

Discover the natural plants of the island and Catalina's history in the tranquil Wrigley Memorial and Botanic Garden.

Outdoor Adventures: Hiking, snorkeling, diving, and zip-lining are all wonderful options in Catalina. Hikers who want to experience the island's wild side should take the Trans-Catalina Trail.

Wildlife Encounters: Keep a look out for the island's resident bison, and take a boat excursion if you want to see dolphins and other marine species.

Historical Sites: Visit places like the Catalina Island Museum and the old Bird Park, which is now a public garden, to learn more about the island's extensive history.

Every type of traveler can find something to enjoy on Catalina Island, including those looking for relaxation as well as adventure seekers and history fans. Discover the many attractions and activities the island has to offer to make the most of your stay.

Chapter 1: 10 Top Attractions

Catalina Island's Avalon Harbor

The gorgeous center of Catalina Island is Avalon Harbor, which is situated on the southeast side. It's a quaint coastal community with a breathtaking seaside location. The harbor is renowned for its energetic vibe, immaculate waters, and lovely promenade. You can engage in a variety of activities here, from unwinding on the beach to discovering the town's eateries and stores.

The famous Casino structure is one of Avalon Harbor's most notable attractions. Despite its name, the Casino is a stunning Art Deco building that houses a theater and a ballroom rather than a place where people can gamble. For its history and architecture, it is a must-see.

Additionally, the harbor serves as a starting point for water sports like boating, scuba diving, and snorkeling. It is a favorite location for underwater aficionados because of the abundance of marine life in the clean waters.

Avalon Harbor is one of Catalina Island's top attractions because it provides a pleasant fusion of leisure, entertainment, and scenic beauty.

Club Descanso Beach

On the beautiful Catalina Island, there lies a magnificent haven called Descanso Beach Club. With its gorgeous beach, cabana rentals, and variety of water sports, it offers a tranquil respite just outside the busy city of Avalon.

Visitors at Descanso Beach Club can unwind on the fine sands, enjoy the warm California sun, and take in the magnificent Pacific Ocean vistas. Rental cabanas at the club provide a sense of exclusivity, complete with devoted staff and facilities.

Adventurers can participate in exhilarating sports like stand-up paddleboarding, kayaking, and even the difficult ropes course Catalina Aerial Adventure.

After a day of exploring the island, the club offers the renowned "Catalina Happy Hour" with live music and delectable cocktails.
Descanso Beach Club is a top destination for visitors looking for a taste of luxury on Catalina Island since it seamlessly blends relaxation and excitement.

Garden of the Wrigley Memorial & Memorial

On Catalina Island, the Wrigley Memorial and Botanic Garden is a fascinating location renowned for both its historical significance and its natural beauty. The garden is a memorial to William Wrigley Jr., the former owner of the island, and is surrounded by a rough landscape.

The actual memorial, which honors Wrigley, is a magnificent building fashioned of local Catalina limestone. It provides sweeping views of the

Pacific Ocean and the island. Through educational exhibits, visitors can learn about the history of the island and the influence of Wrigley.

A treasure mine of rare and indigenous species can be found in the nearby botanic garden. It displays an amazing variety of species, many of which are exclusive to the island. Cacti, succulents, and other types of flora can be found when strolling through the garden's walkways in a tranquil, natural environment.

For history aficionados, nature lovers, and anybody searching for a serene, informative experience on Catalina Island, the Wrigley Memorial and Botanic Garden is a must-visit.

Casino Catalina

On Catalina Island, near the town of Avalon, stands the well-known and recognizable Catalina Casino. Contrary to its name, the "casino" is a multipurpose structure with a colorful past rather than a place where people go to gamble.

William Wrigley Jr. created this spectacular Art Deco structure in 1929, and it is primarily home to a magnificent 1,184-seat theater. Numerous events, including movies, musical concerts, dance performances, and special occasions, have taken place at the theater. The grandiose architecture of the building, along with a magnificent chandelier and moody murals, enhances the overall experience.

The casino also has a large ballroom with an exceptional hardwood dance floor and stunning views of the ocean, which makes it a well-liked location for weddings, galas, and other special events.

The Catalina Casino is a favourite destination for people exploring Avalon since it provides a chance to enjoy the island's history, architecture, and artistic accomplishments.

Three Harbors

On the western side of Catalina Island, in contrast to the busy town of Avalon, is the quaint and isolated location of Two Harbors. Its two bays, Isthmus Cove and Catalina Harbor, which characterize its distinctive terrain, inspired its name.

For those who enjoy the outdoors and the natural world, this place is a heaven. Explore the pristine beaches, stroll beautiful trails, or partake in water sports like kayaking, snorkeling, and boating. Rugged beauty may be seen throughout the environment, with steep cliffs and expansive ocean views.

The historic Banning House Lodge, a charming inn with lovely accommodations, is another highlight in Two Harbors. While enjoying the local natural attractions, it's a great place to stay.

Two Harbors is a must-visit if you're looking for a more sedate and isolated Catalina Island experience. It's remote location and stunning surroundings make it the ideal place to unwind and go on outdoor excursions.

Eco Zipline Tour

The Catalina Island Zip Line Eco Tour is an exhilarating journey that gives you a fresh viewpoint on the island's natural splendor. You travel through the interior of the island on this thrilling trip while perched above the treetops.

Each of the five zip lines that participants soar over offers breath-taking views of the untamed landscape and the Pacific Ocean. A tough suspension bridge is also included in the route, which ups the excitement level.

The Zip Line Eco Tour's eco-friendly philosophy adds to its uniqueness. The tour guides give information about the island's distinct ecosystem, animals, and history, ensuring that visitors have a greater understanding of Catalina's natural splendors.

The Zip Line Eco Tour is an outstanding excursion on Catalina Island, regardless of whether you're an adrenaline addict or just looking to take in the island's breathtaking scenery. In a remarkable way, it mixes the desire for thrills with environmental education.

Ocean Expedition

Catalina Island offers a thrilling Undersea Expedition for people who desire to discover the undiscovered beauties beneath the ocean's surface. This journey offers a rare chance to see the variety of marine life in the pristine seas around the island.

A semi-submersible boat with big viewing windows below the water's surface normally conducts the tour. You'll be treated to a close-up view of kelp forests, brilliant coral reefs, and a variety of colorful fish as you dive into the ocean's depths. Watch out for the Garibaldi, the official marine fish of California, which is frequently seen in these areas.

The Undersea Expedition's skilled guides share unique insights on the island's aquatic ecosystem and the value of conservation. Both nature lovers and families looking for a special trip on

Catalina Island will find it to be an instructive and fascinating experience.

Aviary Park

The Bird Park on Catalina Island is a well-kept secret that provides nature lovers with a tranquil and instructive experience. Originally constructed in 1929, this ancient aviary has recently undergone a stunning restoration. With lovely views of Avalon and the Pacific Ocean, it is situated in a serene hillside area.

Numerous exotic birds, including brightly colored macaws and cockatoos, may be found in Bird Park. Visitors may see and engage with the birds in tranquility thanks to the park's lush vegetation and well-kept enclosures.

The educational exhibits at Bird Park that give details about the island's avian residents and their ecosystems are among its features. It's a great chance to educate yourself on the value of protecting birds and the ecological relevance of Catalina.

For individuals who are passionate about ornithology and wildlife, stopping by Bird Park provides a tranquil respite and the chance to admire the beauty of these wonderful feathered creatures.

The Island Eco Tour

The Island Eco Tour is a great option for a thorough investigation of Catalina Island's natural beauty and different ecosystems. This tour takes you on a journey through the island's interior and provides insights into its history, geology, and fauna under the direction of professional guides.

The journey often include driving across challenging terrain in a cozy open-air car. Ascend to high vantage spots that offer breathtaking panoramic views of the island and the nearby Pacific Ocean as you weave through gorges, meander through eucalyptus trees, and pass through mountainous terrain.

The Island Eco Tour is a learning adventure that explores the island's distinctive flora and animals. While learning about Catalina's natural history and the continuing conservation efforts, you might see bison, island foxes, and a variety of bird species.

For people who enjoy the outdoors and are curious about the ecosystem of the island, this excursion is great. It provides a comprehensive grasp of Catalina's diverse environmental tapestry and is a favourite destination for tourists looking to get in touch with nature.

Museum on Catalina Island

The Catalina Island Museum is a cultural treasure on the island that offers history and art fans a rich and full experience. This museum explores the rich history, art, and culture of Catalina Island and is situated in the center of Avalon.

The museum's displays and holdings give visitors a look into the island's past, from its

Native American roots to its development as a popular tourist destination. It includes many different artifacts, images, and works of art that tell the history of the island.

The history of the Chicago Cubs' spring training on the island is one of the notable exhibits, giving the museum a special sports perspective. There are also displays of local and visiting artists' work.

Anyone who wants to comprehend the island's varied heritage and artistic expression must visit the Catalina Island Museum, which is a trip through time. Your time on Catalina Island will be richer for having visited this center of culture.

Chapter 2: Hidden Gems

Hidden Beaches

Although Catalina Island is well recognized for its beautiful beaches, there are a few lesser-known hidden beauties that are just waiting to be found. One such remote location is Shark Harbor, which is reachable from Two Harbors by a beautiful hike. For those looking for a calm beach experience, this secret cove's peace and privacy make it the ideal getaway.

Ben Weston Beach, a little, secluded paradise found on the western end of the island, is another undiscovered gem. Locals love to keep their beautiful sunsets and quiet waters a secret. To add to the sense of remoteness and adventure that awaits those who seek out these secret pockets of paradise, be sure to bring your own supplies as these beaches may not have the conveniences of the more well-known ones.

Trails for hiking on Catalina Island

With a variety of routes that offer breath-taking panoramas and varied landscapes, Catalina Island is a hiker's paradise. Traveling the 37.2-mile Trans-Catalina Trail will get you from one end of the island to the other and is both difficult and rewarding.

You'll pass through a variety of landscapes along the trip, including undulating hills, untamed woods, and rocky beaches. Try the Hermit Gulch Trail, a moderate 6.5-mile loop with rich foliage, a eucalyptus grove, and panoramic views, for a shorter, undiscovered gem.

You can even find the Garden to Sky Trail, which will take you from the Wrigley Memorial and Botanic Garden to Mount Ada, the island's highest point, giving you a breathtaking view of its splendor. Exploring the hiking trails on Catalina Island is a worthwhile excursion because there are pathways for hikers of all skill levels.

Catalina Island's Island Foxes

The native Island Foxes of Catalina Island are among the island's cutest and most distinctive features. These little animals are a subspecies of gray foxes and are unique to this area of the world. They are regarded as the smallest fox species in North America, weighing only 3-5 pounds.

The population of Catalina Island Foxes has previously suffered considerable difficulties, almost going extinct. Nevertheless, with to conservation efforts, their population has increased once again, making Catalina Island one of the best sites to see these endearing creatures in their native environment.

These inquisitive and amusing animals are frequently seen to tourists, especially in the island's interior. To help safeguard their welfare, keep your distance and prevent from feeding them. It is a wonderful privilege for nature lovers to see the Island Foxes because they are a recognizable component of Catalina's ecosystem.

Scuba Diving on Shipwrecks

Catalina Island is a treasure trove below the surface in addition to being a paradise above the water. Several spectacular shipwrecks are available for scuba divers to explore beneath its crystal-clear waters. The "Suejac" wreck, a gambling ship that sank in the 1930s and is now an artificial reef rich with marine life, is one such noteworthy location.

The "Suejac" wreck is a well-liked destination for scuba divers. As you go down, you'll see the ship's structure still standing and learn how it was transformed into a thriving aquatic habitat. This wreck is home to vibrant fish, sea stars, and anemones, creating a breathtaking underwater display.

The "The Valiant," a 380-foot-long World War II troop transport ship that is currently submerged beneath the seas, is another fantastic diving location. With its gigantic structure covered in kelp and accompanied by a variety of aquatic species, this enormous wreck is both a spooky and exciting experience.

Divers of all experience levels can enjoy a unique and thrilling experience by exploring these shipwrecks, which is like to diving into history. Don't pass up the chance to explore Catalina Island's undiscovered undersea delights.

Campground in Hermit Gulch

Hermit Gulch Campground on Catalina Island is a secret treasure for anyone looking for a fully immersive island experience. This lovely campground offers a rare fusion of accessibility and environment and is only a mile from Avalon.

Hermit Gulch Campground is a great place to pitch a tent or stay in one of their tent cabins because it is surrounded by beautiful scenery and rich greenery. The campgrounds are well-kept and offer a basic but cozy camping experience. You may explore the heart of the island via the lovely Hermit Gulch Trail, which is only a short stroll from the campground.

Hermit Gulch Campground is unique since it is close to Avalon's facilities while still providing a tranquil haven in the wilderness. You may quickly and simply go to the town to eat, shop, or take in the island's attractions.

Hermit Gulch Campground offers a special opportunity to take in Catalina's natural beauty while having the convenience of Avalon close by, whether you're an experienced camper or new to the activity.

Botanical Gardens on Catalina Island

The Catalina Island Botanical Gardens are a secret haven of varied and unusual plant life located in the picturesque interior of Catalina Island. This horticultural treasure highlights the island's abundant biodiversity and provides a tranquil haven for nature lovers.

The 37.5-acre gardens contain a variety of plant species, many of which are unique to the island. Stroll through themed gardens, such as the Channel Islands Section, the Desert Collection, and the peaceful Butterfly Nectar Garden, along well-kept walks. Both botany lovers and those looking for a tranquil and instructive experience will find it to be delightful.

The Wrigley Memorial and Botanic Garden, which features rare and endangered Channel Islands native flora, is one of the attractions. The area also offers stunning views of Avalon and the nearby coastline.

The Catalina Island Botanical Gardens provide an opportunity to engage with the natural history of the island while taking in a peaceful and instructive day in an incredibly picturesque environment.

On Catalina Island, Toyon Bay

On the southwest part of Catalina Island, Toyon Bay is a hidden coastal beauty that is frequently disregarded by tourists. This pristine bay offers a tranquil respite from the commotion of the other tourist destinations.

Toyon Bay's remote position and quiet seas make it a great place for kayaking, swimming, and snorkeling. It is a haven for underwater exploration thanks to its rugged shoreline, abundant marine life, including colorful fish, and kelp forests.

The USC Wrigley Marine Science Center, which focuses on marine life research and instruction, is one distinctive aspect of Toyon Bay. You might have the opportunity to learn about the island's marine ecosystem and its preservation while you're there.

Toyon Bay is a tranquil refuge where you may relax, take part in water sports, and get in touch with nature away from the masses. For visitors seeking a more sedate and off-the-beaten-path experience on Catalina Island, it is a well-kept secret.

Chapter 3: Culinary Delights and Drinks

With its excellent selection of dining options, Catalina Island is a sanctuary for foodies. There is something for everyone, from succulent desserts to fresh fish. The island's cuisine is a unique and mouthwatering experience since it combines California flavors with coastal influences. You may find a variety of food alternatives to tempt your taste buds wherever you go on the island, whether you're strolling downtown Avalon or discovering the more remote areas.

Enjoy the blending of regional and global cuisines that results in a dynamic culinary scene that will leave you wanting more. Catalina Island's culinary culture is a great delight for food lovers, whether it's a laid-back beachside cafe or a fine dining establishment.

Specialty Seafoods

You can enjoy some of the freshest seafood on Catalina Island because of its proximity to the water. Take a bite out of delectable crab, lobster, and fish meals that frequently feature a local touch. Don't miss the famous Catalina Fish Kitchen, a haven for seafood lovers. Enjoy expertly cooked delicacies honoring the island's maritime heritage, such as grilled swordfish or clam chowder.

Visit the Bluewater Avalon for an incredibly real taste of the sea, where the freshest seafood is converted into delectable cuisine that perfectly represent Catalina's seaside beauty. Whether you want your fish fried, grilled, or stewed, Catalina Island's seafood delicacies are a gourmet feast that will take your taste buds right to the ocean.

A View While Eating

Catalina is home to numerous eateries with breathtaking coastal views. Imagine enjoying your dinner while admiring the palm-lined shoreline and blue ocean. It's an encounter that transforms a routine dinner into a noteworthy occasion. The Bluewater Avalon is a favorite pick for dining with a view since it serves delicious seafood and provides expansive harbor views.

Another jewel that lets you eat by the beach with the glistening ocean as your backdrop is Descanso Beach Club. The island's restaurants with views make for a dining experience that isn't just about the food but also about the stunning environment, whether you want to eat during the day or beneath the starry night sky.

Energizing Drinks

Tropical cocktails, regional craft beers, and exquisite wines are just a few of the delicious drinks that the island has to offer. Enjoy a signature mojito at Luau Larry's, where the island's relaxed ambiance is complemented by the tropical tastes. As an alternative, enjoy a glass of wine at the Descanso Beach Club, where you can put your toes in the sand while sipping your beverage.

The pubs and cafes on Catalina Island provide a delicious selection of drinks that are ideal for cooling off and taking in the island's laid-back atmosphere. In this delightful island paradise, whether you choose a traditional margarita or a creative concoction inspired by the island, you'll find cool drinks to fit your taste.

Unusual Island Restaurants

The eccentric and endearing restaurants on Catalina Island contribute to the island's distinctive charm. Discover hidden gems like Steve's Steakhouse for a remarkable dining experience. Here, you may savor a delicious steak in a welcoming setting that captures the warmth of the island. Try Original Jack's Country Kitchen, a lovely diner with an old-school ambiance that serves comfort cuisine that will take you back in time, if you're looking for something genuinely unique.

The restaurants on the island offer a wide range of gastronomic experiences that appeal to a variety of tastes and inclinations. Your dining experience on Catalina will be genuinely memorable thanks to these distinctive island restaurants, which offer not only excellent food but also a dash of regional history and personality.

As the sun sets, eat

In Catalina, sunset dinners are a necessity. Enjoy a delicious supper as you watch the sun dip behind the horizon. The Lobster Trap is one of the most beautiful locations for a sunset supper. While feasting in fresh seafood and other culinary treats, diners can take in the bright colors of a Catalina sunset in this restaurant's beautiful location.

The restaurants on the island offer the ideal setting for a romantic or peaceful eating experience as the sun paints the sky in orange and pink tones. You won't soon forget the experience of dining while taking in one of Catalina's magnificent sunsets.

Desserts and other sweets

Don't forget to indulge in some of Catalina's delicious sweets to satiate your sweet taste. The Pancake Cottage is a well-known location to eat delectable pancakes, whether you prefer them with fresh fruit, chocolate chips, or maple syrup drizzled over top. Visit Lloyd's of Avalon for a delectable array of ice cream flavors and delicious snacks. There, you may make your own sundaes or take pleasure in a traditional cone on a warm day.

As varied and opulent as the island's savory food are its dessert alternatives. Catalina makes sure your meal ends on a sweet note with everything from time-honored favorites to creative confections. Save room for dessert and discover the amazing world of sweets that this lovely island has to offer.

Chapter 4: Restaurants and Costs

Eateries Avalon

The largest town on Catalina Island, Avalon, provides a wide variety of food alternatives to suit different preferences and price ranges. You'll find something to sate your cravings, from fresh seafood to American favorites.

Avalon restaurants: Avalon is home to a variety of quaint seaside restaurants, some of which have breath-taking ocean views. Local seafood is available at restaurants such Bluewater Avalon and The Lobster Trap. Armstrong's Fish Market and Steve's Steakhouse are excellent options if you enjoy American cuisine. Try Luau Larry's, famed for its tropical beverages, for a relaxed ambiance. Everyone can find something they like at Avalon in terms of the ambiance and food variety.

Two Harbors Restaurant

On Catalina Island, Two Harbors is a smaller, more private neighborhood, yet it still has wonderful dining options. Visit the Harbor Reef Restaurant for a casual supper, where you may enjoy traditional American fare while seeing the harbor. It's the ideal place to unwind because of its beachfront location.

Doug's Harbor Reef is another choice to take into account if you're in the mood for some seafood. In a casual environment, they provide the day's freshest fish.

One of the best places to enjoy a dinner and take in the natural beauty of the island is Two Harbors because of its reputation for tranquility and calm.

Cost-effective options

Catalina Island provides options for individuals looking for inexpensive dining options. Several possibilities are:

Antonio's Pizzeria & Cabaret: This establishment serves pizza and Italian food and has an affordable menu in a relaxed atmosphere.

On the Pier, Eric It's a terrific place for good yet affordable meals, especially when you eat on the pier and it's known for its fish and chips.

Avalon's Lloyd's: A popular among locals for breakfast and lunch that offers filling quantities at reasonable prices.

Additionally, there are informal cafes and food trucks that offer options without breaking the bank. A cheap way to enjoy meals and the stunning surroundings of the island is by exploring local markets and picnicking.

Experiments in Fine Dining

Catalina Island has some outstanding fine dining establishments as well as casual dining options. These restaurants serve superb food in a posh setting:

Avalon's Bluewater Grill is a classy beachfront eatery known for its seafood. Dishes like

Macadamia Nut-Crusted Mahi-Mahi and Grilled Swordfish are served here.

The Avalon Grille, a restaurant in the center of Avalon, mixes a contemporary setting with traditional fare, offering a variety of mouthwatering choices such Filet Mignon and Wild Mushroom Risotto.
For those in search of a substantial steak, Steve's Steakhouse provides premium cuts in a cozy atmosphere.

Offering a taste of luxury on the island, these fine dining venues make the ideal environment for a memorable occasion or a romantic supper.

Breakfast places and cafés

Catalina Island has delightful locations where you can start your day with a hearty breakfast or a warm cup of coffee. Here are a few well-liked choices:
Coffee & Cookie Company of Catalina: The friendly café in Avalon is a favorite among

coffee enthusiasts. Enjoy a variety of delectable sweets and pastries with your beverage.

Pancakes, omelets, and fresh cinnamon rolls are among the basic American breakfast options available at Original Jack's Country Kitchen, a vintage restaurant.

The Pancake home offers a range of flavors and toppings for its pancakes, as the name of this quaint home suggests.

Before setting off on island activities, you can have your breakfast meal in a laid-back setting at these locations.

Vegetarian and Vegan Options

There are options for vegans and vegetarians on Catalina Island, which is famous for its seafood and pork dishes. Among the places to see are:

Veggie burgers and salads are available at Coyote Joe's in Avalon, a relaxed restaurant.

A delightful cafe serving vegan and vegetarian food, including a vegan breakfast burrito and salads, is called Cafe Metropole.

The vegetarian menu at Bluewater Grill includes dishes like the Grilled Vegetable Plate and Wild Mushroom Risotto.

While the island's main emphasis is on seafood, these eateries provide options for individuals who prefer plant-based eating.

Typical Meal Prices

A variety of dining alternatives are available on Catalina Island to suit various price ranges. Here is a broad notion of how much you should budget for a supper at different kinds of establishments:

Budget-kind Options: Meals cost between $10 and $20 per person at restaurants that are kind to your wallet.

Fine Dining Experiences: The average cost per person at a fine dining establishment ranges from $50 to $100 or more, depending on your preferences.

Cafés and Breakfast Locations: The average cost of breakfast and café meals is between $10 and $20 per person.

Prices for vegan and vegetarian selections can vary, however they are frequently comparable to the average cost of a restaurant of that sort.

It's crucial to remember that costs can change depending on the restaurant and the meals you order. On Catalina Island, several restaurants also serve prix fixe menus, which can set a fixed price for multi-course meals.

Chapter 5: Transportation and Costs

How to Navigate Catalina Island

There are many ways to get around Catalina Island, which is off the coast of Southern California, so that you may discover its scenic landscapes and quaint communities. Renting a golf cart is one of the most common ways to move around. You can tour the island at your own leisure by renting one of the many golf carts that are readily available. It's an enjoyable and practical method to explore the area and enjoy the beautiful scenery.

To get to the island from the mainland more quickly, you can use the Catalina Express Ferry or Island Express Helicopter services. Once on Catalina, buses offer a convenient method to explore the area around Avalon. Shopping, dining, and activities are all conveniently located within walking distance of one another in this charming town.

I'd be pleased to provide you more information, including pricing and transportation suggestions.

Rentals for golf carts

Renting a golf cart is a classic and fun way to see Catalina Island. Both locals and visitors like to use these compact electric cars. They offer a distinctive and relaxing experience as you go through the quaint streets of Avalon and explore the picturesque interior of the island.

There are several rental companies in Avalon where you may rent golf carts, but it's a good idea to make a reservation in advance, especially during the busiest travel times. The carts normally come in a variety of sizes that can hold two, four, or even six people. Depending on the size and length of your rental, prices change.

Remember that golf carts can only be used in a few places on the island, namely Avalon, so if you want to tour farther-flung areas, you might want to think about taking another mode of transportation. However, hiring a golf cart is a great way to experience Catalina Island's laid-back atmosphere.

helicopter service Island Express

If you want to get to Catalina Island quickly and thrillingly, think about using the Island Express Helicopter service. This choice gives you a distinctive view of the island's magnificent vistas and a practical means to get where you're going. The helicopter service is available from the mainland, typically from Long Beach or San Pedro airports.

The helicopter flight offers breathtaking overhead views of Catalina's rough landscape and the Pacific Ocean. Particularly enticing to people with limited availability or seeking a premium experience is the ease of a quicker journey.

A dependable option for transportation to the island, Island Express Helicopter is renowned for its punctuality and safety standards. However, have in mind that it is more expensive than using the boat, so while deciding how to get to Catalina Island, take your preferences and budget into account.

Ferry Catalina Express

For getting to Catalina Island from the Southern California mainland, the Catalina Express Ferry is a well-liked and economical option. This ferry service provides frequent voyages to the island's Avalon and Two Harbors, departing from a number of ports including Long Beach, San Pedro, and Dana Point.

During the roughly hour-long trip, the ferry offers passengers beautiful ocean vistas and the chance to see aquatic life. Given that the rates are reasonably priced and the boat can carry a sizable number of passengers, it's a practical alternative, especially for tourists traveling in big groups or with children.

Catalina Express is adaptable to fit into your schedule because it offers a variety of departure times throughout the day. Most visitors going to Catalina Island prefer to use this ferry service due to its accessibility and convenience.

Transportation by bus

Once you've arrived on Catalina Island, you can use the local bus transit system to tour the island's sights and scenic areas. The island's largest city, Avalon, provides an efficient bus service that runs inside the city and to adjacent tourist attractions.

The main modes of public transportation are the Catalina Trolley and Catalina Transit buses. They are quick and economical methods to get around Avalon and stop at famous places like the Casino or the Wrigley Memorial and Botanic Garden.

The island takes precautions to protect its natural beauty, thus these buses are not only useful but also environmentally sustainable. Since many of the sights in Avalon are close to one another, strolling is a terrific choice for tourists who prefer a slower pace.

You might require other transportation, such as a golf cart or guided excursions, if you intend to travel further into the heart of the island or visit less accessible regions.

Tips for Transportation

Here are some crucial transportation suggestions for exploring Catalina Island to make your trip more pleasurable:

Plan Ahead: Take into account your available transportation alternatives and make reservations if necessary, especially during the busiest travel times.

Golf Carts: Read over the rules and conditions of the rental agreement if you're hiring a golf cart. They are a fantastic way to discover Avalon.

Choose between the Catalina Express Ferry and the Island Express Helicopter based on your schedule and financial constraints. Both provide distinctive experiences.

If you intend to use Avalon's public transit, consult the bus timetable. Buses are practical and reasonably priced.

Walking: Considering how many sites are nearby each other, exploring Avalon on foot is a great experience.

Travel with eco-consciousness and show respect for the island's conservation efforts by reducing your environmental effect.

Dress appropriately: Be ready for a variety of weather because the island's climate can change quickly.

Timeliness: To ensure a seamless voyage, arrive early for ferry or helicopter departures.

You'll navigate Catalina Island easily and enjoyably if you abide by these recommendations.

Costs of Transportation

Depending on the mode of transportation and your personal preferences, transportation prices on Catalina Island can vary. Here is a broad breakdown of transportation expenses:

Rental golf carts: Depending on the size and length of the rental, prices might range from $40 to $90 per hour. An entire day's rental may cost between $120 and $200.

In general, one-way helicopter costs start at roughly $135 per person, according to Island Express Helicopter. There are round-trip packages available that provide some financial savings.

The ferry, operated by Catalina Express, is one of the less expensive choices. Adult one-way tickets range from $37 to $76, depending on your point of departure. Discounts are frequently given to elders and children.

Bus: In Avalon, one-way bus fares normally cost around $2 per person. The local bus service is very affordable.

It's a good idea to check with the specific transportation providers for the most recent pricing and any special offers because rates are subject to change at any time. Additionally, you can maximize your transportation spending in Catalina Island by taking into account variables like group discounts or package deals.

Chapter 6: Accommodations and Costs

Off the coast of Southern California, Catalina Island has a wide variety of lodging options to enhance your island experience.

Hotels and Resorts by Avalon

The major city on the island, Avalon, has a variety of hotels and resorts. There are accommodations for every type of traveler, from opulent luxury hotels with seaside views to quaint boutique inns. Prices in Avalon will likely increase, especially during the peak season. To guarantee your chosen choice, it is advisable to book reservations well in advance.

Three Harbors Inn

Two Harbors is the area to look at for lodging options if you're searching for a more isolated and natural experience on Catalina Island.

The west end of the island, where Two Harbors is situated, has a calmer and more natural atmosphere. Here are a few places to stay in Two Harbors:

Rentals of cabins: Cozy cabins with the essentials are available for rent. These cabins frequently offer a more secluded and adventurous kind of stay.

Camping: There are campgrounds in Two Harbors where you may set up a tent and take in the great outdoors. Prioritize reservations, especially during the busy season.

Consider boat-in camping for a distinctive adventure in the secluded coves of the island. It's a fantastic way to get a close-up view of Catalina's natural splendor.

For those wanting a peaceful and natural escape, Two Harbors is perfect. It might not be as opulent as some Avalon lodgings, but its tranquil atmosphere and close accessibility to outdoor activities more than make up for it. Plan early, especially if you're thinking of renting a cabin or going camping.

Catalina Island Camping Options

Camping on Catalina Island is a great opportunity to see its breathtaking natural beauty firsthand. Consider these possibilities for camping:

There are a number of campgrounds available in Two Harbors, including Two Harbors Campground and Little Harbor Campground.

Reservations are strongly advised, especially during the peak season, as these sites offer a modest camping experience with little amenities. Avalon campgrounds: For people who desire to explore the town and its activities, Avalon also includes campgrounds. One such campground is Hermit Gulch Campground. Here, too, bookings in advance are important.

Parson's Landing Campground: You may reach this campground by kayak or a moderately difficult hike. It's a peaceful, picturesque location that's ideal for a more private camping trip.

Consider boat-in camping at numerous coves around the island for the ultimate getaway. This alternative offers a special and exclusive camping vacation but calls for planning and permits.

The campgrounds on Catalina Island provide a variety of camping experiences, from rustic camping near Avalon to more modern options. Remember that camping on the island is very popular, thus reservations must be made much in advance, especially if you intend to camp at the busiest time of year.

Holiday Rentals

Vacation rentals are a terrific alternative to typical hotels if you're searching for a more independent and local experience while visiting Catalina Island. What you need to know is as follows:

Different Rentals: Apartments, condos, cottages, and homes are available for short-term rentals on the island. You can choose from quaint couple's getaways to roomier family lodgings depending on your group size and interests.

Local Experience: Staying in a vacation rental enables you to become fully immersed in the neighborhood and culture, providing a more genuine sense of the island.

Amenities & Privacy: The majority of vacation rentals have fully functional kitchens, making it easy to prepare meals. In comparison to hotels, you'll frequently experience more privacy.

Booking: Vacation homes on Catalina Island are listed on a number of websites, including Airbnb and Vrbo. Make sure to reserve early, especially during busy travel times.

Rentals are offered in both Avalon and Two Harbors, providing a variety of location options.

If you want a home-away-from-home experience, vacation rentals can be a great option. They are frequently more affordable, especially for longer stays or larger groups.

Make sure to shop around and reserve a rental that fits both your demands and your budget.

Tips for lodging

Here are some helpful hints to make the most of your Catalina Island accommodations:

In advance bookings: Make reservations far in advance, especially during the busiest travel season, whether you're reserving a hotel room, a vacation home, or a campsite. This guarantees you a place to stay and might even result in a financial benefit.

Pack appropriately: Pack the right supplies, such as sleeping bags, cooking utensils, and camping necessities, if you plan to go camping or stay in more basic accommodations.

Weekday Stays: Instead of scheduling your trip for the weekend, give midweek a thought. During the week, a lot of lodgings offer discounted prices and packages to help you cut expenditures.

Package offers: Seek out lodgings that provide bundle offers that combine staying with well-liked island activities like zip-lining, snorkeling, or guided excursions. These have a lot of potential worth.

Transportation: Verify that getting to and from the island is part of your lodging arrangements. Ferry or helicopter transportation is included in some hotel and package arrangements.

Off-Peak Season: If your trip dates are open, consider visiting during this time of year. You'll not only get greater deals, but the environment will be quieter as well.

These pointers will help you get the most out of your time on Catalina Island while staying within your means and ensuring a hassle-free stay.

Costs of Hostels

You may get the most of your trip by carefully planning it by being aware of the prices related to lodging in Catalina Island. What you need to know is this:

Avalon Price: The largest settlement on the island, Avalon, has more expensive lodging alternatives than Two Harbors or camping. Property on the oceanfront and upscale resorts will cost more.

Campgrounds and Two Harbors: The hotel and camping options in Two Harbors are often more affordable. It is perfect for those on a limited budget because cabin rentals and campgrounds offer affordable options.

Rentals for holidays: The price of a vacation rental varies according to the size, location, and amenities of the property. From more affordable cottages to luxurious waterfront properties, there are alternatives available for different price ranges.

Periodic Pricing: The time of year has a big impact on price. The busiest time of year is summer, when prices are highest. Traveling off-peak can result in big financial savings.

Special Packages: Search for lodging deals that come with extra activities or services. These packages might offer savings by combining housing with well-liked island activities.

Additional Fees: If you're camping, be aware that there may be additional expenses like cleaning fees, resort fees, or equipment rentals.

Finding the perfect lodging that meets your budgetary needs while still allowing you to take advantage of all that Catalina Island has to offer will be made easier if you are aware of the pricing variations and plan your trip in accordance with your budget.

Maintaining a Budget

Although Catalina Island has a variety of lodging options, you may still have a wonderful time there on a budget. Here are some ideas for remaining within your means:

When to Go: Off-Peak Season Typically, lodging costs are lower when traveling during the shoulder or off-peak season. To find better prices, go throughout the fall or spring.

Discover Camping: A cost-effective option to take in the island's natural beauty is to go camping. Campgrounds in Two Harbors and Avalon are available in a range of price points.

Vacation rentals: Take into account accommodations with kitchens. This enables you to cook your own meals, which lowers your eating bills.

Mid-Week Stays: Many lodgings provide discounts for stays during the middle of the week. If possible, book your appointment for Monday through Thursday.

Package Deals: Seek out lodging that includes activities or transportation as part of the deal. These may result in financial savings.

BYO Gear: If you're going camping, try to bring your own supplies. Renting out equipment may increase your costs.

Use Public Transportation: For reasonably priced transportation while on the island, think about taking the Catalina Island Conservancy shuttle.

You may enjoy Catalina Island without going overboard if you use these cost-effective suggestions. Plan ahead and benefit from offers and discounts when they become available.

Chapter 7: 7 Days Itinerary

Day 1: Avalon exploration

Your seven-day adventure gets off to a wonderful start in Avalon, the charming Catalina Island entryway. Walk around Crescent Avenue in the morning; it is lined with quaint stores and eateries. Discover the legendary Catalina Casino, a marvel of Art Deco, and possibly see a movie or go on the Behind the Scenes Tour. The picturesque Descanso Beach is a must-see, where you can unwind on the sand or try water sports like kayaking and snorkeling.

Enjoy some delicious fresh fish for lunch at one of Avalon's seaside restaurants. Visit the serene, native-plant-filled Wrigley Memorial & Botanic Garden in the late afternoon. Take a sunset sail to round off the day and take in the beauty of the island as the sun sets.

Avalon's blend of natural beauty and historic charm creates the ideal setting for an unforgettable Catalina vacation.

Day 2: Watersports and Beach Activities

The focus of day two is enjoying Catalina Island's water splendors. After a full breakfast in the morning, drive to Descanso Beach to begin your day with a range of water sports. To explore the fascinating underwater world, you can hire paddle boards, kayaks, or even give snorkeling a shot.

Make your way to Lover's Cove, a marine park, for a relaxing afternoon where you may snorkel and see the marine life and colorful fish. Consider signing up for a guided scuba diving tour if you want to explore the island's underwater splendor further.

Relax with a drink at one of the beachside bars in the evening, and if you're lucky, you might witness a stunning sunset. After day two, you'll have a deeper understanding of Catalina's marine wonders and the peace that comes from being near the water.

Day 3: Adventures in Hiking

On day three, when you go out on a hiking adventure, Catalina Island's natural splendor truly shines. After a filling breakfast, start your day by going to the trailhead for the hike of your choice. From the picturesque Garden to Sky Trail to more difficult options like the Trans-Catalina Trail, the island has a variety of paths appropriate for hikers of all skill levels.

You'll be surrounded by stunning landscapes, challenging terrain, and a wide variety of flora and fauna while you hike. Watch out for the island's indigenous bison, a fascinating sight to behold. Think of packing a picnic to enjoy in the untainted wildness of the island.

If you decide to remain overnight, unwind and revitalize after your hike at one of Catalina's lovely resorts or the island's campgrounds. You can connect with the island's wild side during this day of exploration and learn about its untamed beauty.

Exploration of Two Harbors on Day 4

Go to the lesser-known treasure of Two Harbors on the fourth day of your Catalina Island vacation. Take the picturesque ferry from Avalon to Two Harbors to start your day off with views of the island's rocky coastline.

You'll be enchanted by Two Harbors' serenity and rural charm the moment you arrive. Visit the Isthmus Cove first, where you can rent paddle boards, go snorkeling, or just unwind on the beach. Enjoy a delicious lunch at the Harbor Reef Restaurant, which is renowned for its excellent seafood.

Take a guided Jeep tour around the interior of the island in the late afternoon to learn more about the particular ecosystem and history of Catalina. Alternately, go for a hike along the western coast of the island and savor the breathtaking views.

As the day draws to a close, savor a tranquil evening by the waterfront while taking in Two Harbors' quiet ambiance, which provides a closer look at Catalina's natural splendor.

Day Five: Outdoor Activities

The focus of day five is expanding your horizons and appreciating Catalina's outdoor pursuits. After a substantial breakfast, start your day with the Zip Line Eco Tour, where you'll soar into the air while viewing the island's stunning scenery as you pass through gorges and through trees.

After your heart-pounding adventure, take a quick trek to the tranquil Wrigley Memorial & Botanic Garden, where you may unwind and discover the island's indigenous plants. Enjoy a lunchtime picnic amidst the lovely grounds.

Take an off-road vehicle excursion in the afternoon to explore Catalina's interior, which will take you over tough terrain and to secret locations on the island. For an alternative view of the island's sceneries, think about riding a horse.

You can retell your day's events while enjoying dinner at one of Avalon's beautiful eateries. On day five, you can participate in a wide variety of outdoor pursuits that will give you a long-lasting sense of adventure.

Day 6: Relaxed and healthy

Day six of your Catalina Island vacation is all about unwinding and taking care of your health. Start your day with a morning yoga session on the sand and let the soothing sound of the waves calm your spirit.

After your yoga session, reward yourself with a day at an opulent health facility on the island where you may indulge in massages, facials, and other restorative services. Numerous spas use regional ingredients and methods to provide distinctive Catalina experiences.

At one of the island's wellness-focused eateries with fresh and organic options for lunch, choose a nutritious meal. Spend the afternoon taking a leisurely stroll along the beach, looking for seashells or just enjoying the fresh sea air.

Enjoy a fine dining experience in Avalon in the evening while indulging in fresh seafood and locally produced foods to ensure that your wellness-focused day comes to a gratifying conclusion. Day six is your chance to relax and re-establish contact with who you are, leaving you feeling rejuvenated.

Day 7: Island Goodbye

Take use of the time you have left on your last day in Catalina. Enjoy a leisurely breakfast at a neighborhood café to start your day and sample the island's distinctive cuisine.

Take one final stroll along Avalon's waterfront, perhaps purchasing a few trinkets or presents from the quaint stores. To learn more about the history and culture of the island, you can also go to the Catalina Island Museum.

Enjoy a seafood feast at one of the restaurants on the oceanfront as you say goodbye and reflect on your amazing week spent on Catalina Island.

Consider taking a glass-bottom boat tour to get one more look at the undersea world before you leave. Take a minute to admire the island's beauty as the sun sets on your final day there and consider taking some special shots to treasure.

Your seven-day schedule on Catalina Island comes to a successful conclusion with the ideal balance of discovery, leisure, and enduring memories. You'll take Catalina's magic with you when you say goodbye to this island paradise and look forward to seeing it again soon.

Chapter 8: Shopping and Markets

Gift Shops

Catalina Island offers a great assortment of souvenir shops that are perfect for capturing the flavor of your visit. These shops are distributed over the island, with popular selections like "Catalina Treasures" and "Island Shop" located along Crescent Avenue. You'll find a wide choice of souvenirs, including T-shirts, postcards, mugs, and unusual island-themed presents.

These stores cater to both tourists and locals, assuring you'll find something to remember your Catalina Island trip. Whether you're shopping for a keepsake to memorialize your vacation or a gift for friends and family back home, these souvenir shops provide something for everyone. Don't forget to explore the quaint tiny boutiques and art stores nearby, which typically sell one-of-a-kind goods that embody the island's particular appeal.

Local crafts and art

A lively arts and crafts community that is strongly ingrained in the local culture may be found on Catalina Island. The island is home to many gifted artists, whose work is displayed in numerous galleries and studios. The island's natural beauty and coastal surroundings served as inspiration for a wide variety of art forms, including handcrafted jewelry, finely created pottery, intriguing paintings, and exquisite sculptures.

It's possible to bring a piece of Catalina's artistic energy home with you by exploring the local art and craft sector in addition to appreciating the islanders' inventiveness. You can explore these distinctive works of art at galleries like "Avalon Glass Art" or "Catalina Pottery" and perhaps discover a piece that speaks to your personal taste and memories of the island.

Market in Catalina Island for farmers

For those looking for locally produced, fresh food and handcrafted goods, the Catalina Island Farmers Market is a wonderful place to visit. This market, which is only held sometimes, usually in the summer, brings together regional farmers, craftspeople, and food vendors to highlight the best of the island's agricultural products.

Explore the market to find a variety of fresh fruits, vegetables, and herbs, many of which are produced on the island itself. Additionally, you can buy specialty handcrafted items that are ideal for gifts and souvenirs, such as honey, preserves, and home-baked goods.

The market offers a wonderful chance to get to know the locals and experience Catalina's culinary offerings. A trip to the Catalina Island Farmers Market is a must-do activity while you're on the island, whether you're a foodie or just trying to get a feel for the community. When you visit, be sure to check the schedule for the dates and times of the market.

Shops in boutiques

The charming boutique shops on Catalina Island provide a special and carefully curated shopping experience. You'll find a variety of boutique stores that appeal to a wide range of tastes as you stroll through the charming streets of Avalon, especially along Crescent Avenue.

These shops typically stock carefully chosen apparel, accessories, and other unusual items. Whether you're looking for trendy clothing, beachwear, or unique goods with island themes, you're certain to find hidden gems in these shops. The Shop at the Atwater and Island Threadz are two popular choices.

The opportunity to find things that capture the style and personality of the island is a benefit of shopping in these boutiques.

The stores on Catalina Island offer a variety of choices, from casual clothing for a day at the beach to chic evening dress, making your shopping experience pleasurable and gratifying. Don't forget to browse the boutiques while you're there to see what catches your attention.

Gems and Jewelry

For individuals who value exquisite craftsmanship and one-of-a-kind pieces, Catalina Island has a wonderful collection of jewelry and gems. Coastal scenery and the island's natural splendor serve as inspiration for numerous jewelers and craftspeople. Consider perusing the jewelry shops on Catalina Island while seeking for a thoughtful present or a particular keepsake.

You can find gorgeous items with a range of jewels, many of which have hues similar to those of the ocean, such as turquoise and pearls. These stones are painstakingly combined into rings, necklaces, bracelets, and earrings to produce creations that perfectly depict the beauty of the island.

You can browse and select from a variety of possibilities by going to jewelry stores like "Catalina Island Jewelry" or "Two Harbors Island Supply". These shops offer a varied range to accommodate various preferences and budgets, whether you're looking for a classic piece or a one-of-a-kind design. So, if you want to bring something lovely and distinctive from Catalina Island home, you must visit the jewelry and gem shops.

Shopper Advice

Keep the following pointers in mind when shopping on Catalina Island to maximize your retail therapy experience:

Make a plan: Make a list of the things you wish to buy or look into, whether they be trinkets, works of art, outfits, or jewelry. Making the most of your time and maintaining attention may both be accomplished with a strategy.

Smart Spending: Catalina Island is a popular tourist destination, thus costs can go up. Create a budget to prevent overspending.

Check for Sales: Many stores periodically offer discounts and specials. Pay attention to sales and promotions, especially at off-peak times.

Crescent Avenue is the main commercial center, but don't be afraid to explore the side streets and alleys as well. You can come upon boutique shops and undiscovered gems.

Request recommendations from locals: Locals frequently know firsthand where to find the greatest stores. Don't be afraid to ask locals or other tourists for recommendations.

Put on comfy Shoes: You'll probably be walking a lot, so comfy shoes are essential.

Respect Store Hours: Be mindful of the opening and closing times of businesses and markets, as these can vary depending on the season.

By keeping these shopping ideas in mind, you can enjoy a more enjoyable and profitable shopping experience during your visit to Catalina Island.

Market Times

You must schedule your shopping according to the various markets' and establishments' operating hours on Catalina Island. Here is a general rule of thumb:

Especially during the busiest travel seasons, souvenir shops are often open during the day and into the early evening. Some might work longer hours.

Local art and crafts: Art studios and galleries typically have set business hours. The schedules of the galleries you plan to see should be checked in advance.

Catalina Island Farmers Market: The market may have set days and times, however it typically operates throughout the summer. The most recent information can be found by checking local listings or by contacting the visitor center.

Generally speaking, Avalon's boutique shops operate within standard business hours, opening in the morning and closing in the evening. Those who work off-season hours might change them. Jewelry and gems shops typically operate throughout regular business hours, just like boutique stores, but it's a good idea to double-check with each particular store.

It is advisable to contact the businesses or the Catalina Island Chamber of Commerce for the most up-to-date details on their opening times while you are there. Making the most of your shopping time on the island can be accomplished by planning beforehand.

Chapter 9: Health and Safety Information

Emergency numbers

Having the correct contact information is essential in case of emergency on Catalina Island:

911: In any emergency, phone 911 for quick assistance. This will link you up with the necessary neighborhood services.

Station of the Sheriff on Catalina Island: The Catalina Island Sheriff's Station can be reached at (310) 510-0174 for non-emergencies or to speak with the local police.

While exploring the island, be sure to store these phone numbers to your phone or have them nearby. Knowing how to get assistance in the event of any unanticipated circumstances is crucial because your safety and well-being are our top priorities.

Medical Services

For the benefit of visitors' health, Catalina Island offers the following medical services:
The main hospital on the island, Catalina Island Medical Center, is in Avalon and provides primary care, urgent care, and a pharmacy. Their phone number is (310) 510-0700.

Although the island is typically safe, mishaps and small health problems can still happen. It is a good idea to be familiar with the Catalina Island Medical Center's location and phone number. This institution is well-equipped to offer the essential support in the event of a medical emergency or healthcare need while you are visiting.

On Catalina Island, staying safe

A pleasant trip to Catalina Island depends on your safety there:
When hiking or exploring the island's wilderness, stay on designated trails and roads.

Going off the beaten path can be dangerous and harmful to the ecosystem.

Observe the Signs: Pay attention to the signs and notifications that are placed since they include important information about potential dangers, animal habitats, and prohibited places.

Cliff Protection Keep an eye out for cliffs and inclining ground. Avoid getting too close to edges to avoid mishaps.

Awareness of the weather Before engaging in outside activities, check the weather forecast. It is advisable to dress in layers because the weather on Catalina Island is erratic.

You can explore the island's natural beauty in a safe and enjoyable manner by paying attention to these safety recommendations.

Safety in the water on Catalina Island

On Catalina Island, water sports are common, however it's important to put safety first when having fun in the water:

Use the right equipment: Whether you're swimming, snorkeling, kayaking, or taking part in other water sports, make sure you have the right tools.

Currents & Tides: Be mindful of the tidal patterns and current conditions. These are subject to daily change, which has an impact on water safety.

Life vests: Wear a life jacket when it is suitable, especially if you have trouble swimming or are in an area with strong currents.

friend System: Engage in aquatic activities with a friend whenever possible. It's more pleasurable and safer.

Respect Marine Life: Marine life abounds in Catalina's waters. Respect the aquatic life by not touching or disturbing it.

These safety measures will help guarantee a fun and safe swimming experience on Catalina Island.

Catalina Island's sun protection

You should use sun protection because of the island's hot, sunny climate:

Sunscreen: Cover exposed skin on your face, neck, and limbs with a broad-spectrum sunscreen with a high SPF rating. Regularly reapply, particularly after swimming.

Hats: A wide-brimmed hat can offer additional protection for your face and neck from the sun.

Invest in UV-protective eyewear to safeguard your eyes from the damaging rays of the sun.

Lightweight clothing can help protect you from the sun, especially during the hottest parts of the day.

Shade: When feasible, seek refuge in areas that are shaded, particularly during the warmest times of the day.

By adhering to these sun safety recommendations, you may take advantage of Catalina Island's lovely weather while reducing your risk of skin cancer and sunburn.

Animal Safety on Catalina Island

Although most of the species on Catalina Island is not dangerous, it is nevertheless vital to respect and be aware of them:

Keeping a Safe Distance: If you come across any animals, such as foxes, birds, or bison, keep a safe distance and observe them. Never approach them or try to feed them.

Bird Nesting locations: If you enjoy watching birds, you should be aware of nesting locations. To safeguard the island's bird population, avoid interfering with breeding locations.

Hiking Safety: To prevent causing as much damage as possible to the island's ecology and animals, hike only on approved pathways.

Avoid touching or bothering marine life when snorkeling or scuba diving. Enjoy the underwater environment without harming anything.

Waste Management: To stop wildlife from being drawn to your picnic or camping spot, properly dispose of your rubbish.

The distinct biodiversity of Catalina Island contributes to its appeal. You support their preservation and the island's ecosystem by treating indigenous animals with respect and living in harmony with them.

Catalina Island Travel Insurance

When preparing for your trip to Catalina Island, keep the following in mind regarding travel insurance:

Coverage Requirements: Make sure that medical emergencies, trip cancellations, and interruptions are covered by your travel insurance.

Coverage Specific to an Island: Check to see if your insurance expressly covers demands and activities on Catalina Island, such as water sports, travel, and distinctive island experiences. Check your insurance coverage to see if emergency evacuation from the island is covered.

Earlier Conditions: To make sure you have sufficient coverage, let your insurer know if you have any pre-existing medical issues.

Policy Specifics: Recognize the requirements of your travel insurance coverage, including how to submit claims and who to contact for help.

Having thorough travel insurance can provide you peace of mind, particularly when visiting far-off places like Catalina Island. It guarantees your safety in the event of unforeseen circumstances while you are traveling.

Chapter 10: Cultural Experiences and Festivals

The rich history and thriving community of Catalina Island are reflected in the diverse range of cultural experiences and festivals that the island provides. You are welcomed by a Mediterranean-inspired atmosphere as soon as you get off the ferry, which sets the setting for an unforgettable stay.

The historic Catalina Casino, a stunning Art Deco structure holding a theater and museum, can be explored as part of the island's cultural experiences. It serves as a focus for cultural events like concerts and film festivals.

Catalina offers numerous annual festivals and events that are integral to its culture. For instance, the Avalon Ball, a lavish dance extravaganza in the style of the 1920s, pays homage to the island's heyday as a glitzy vacation spot. With parades and other events, the

Buccaneer Days Festival honors the island's history of pirates.

These cultural events and celebrations provide a lovely window into Catalina Island's distinctive personality.

Hawaiian Culture

The culture of Catalina Island is a unique fusion of leisure, outdoor exploration, and a hint of Mediterranean flair. The calmer pace of life on the island makes it a great getaway for people looking to escape the hustle and bustle of the mainland.

The architecture of the island, with its quaint pastel structures and Spanish-inspired style, adds to its distinctive personality. The main city on the island, Avalon, has a laid-back, seaside vibe that you may experience by meandering through the streets.

The appreciation of the outdoors and natural beauty is important to island culture. There is a strong connection to the ocean, and kayaking, scuba diving, and other water sports are very popular. You may embrace the daring side of Catalina's culture by hiking, zip-lining, and exploring the untamed interior of the island.

The island's culinary sector also offers a blend of tastes, fusing indigenous delicacies with fresh fish. Dining in Catalina offers the chance to appreciate the cuisine and culture that contribute to this island's uniqueness as a travel destination.

Galleries of art

The art culture on Catalina Island is growing, with many galleries presenting a wide variety of artistic mediums. These galleries serve as venues for both local and visiting artists to display their work in addition to being locations to enjoy art.

The Catalina Island Art Association's Galleria is one noteworthy location. The diverse collection of artwork in this gallery was produced by gifted regional artists. The island's distinctive scenery and marine life are frequently used as inspiration for paintings, sculptures, and other types of visual art. The Catalina community's brilliance and ingenuity can be seen by exploring the Galleria.

In addition to the Galleria, Avalon is dotted with smaller, independent galleries, each of which offers a unique perspective on artistic study. These locations offer chances to interact with artists, buy original artwork, and get a taste of Catalina Island's creative energy. The art galleries on Catalina are an important component of the island's cultural landscape, whether you're a seasoned art enthusiast or just looking for creative inspiration.

Museums and displays

The remarkable collection of museums and galleries on Catalina Island offers tourists insightful information about the island's past, distinctive environment, and rich cultural legacy.

A vital cultural site is the Catalina Island Museum. It acts as a window into the island's past, illustrating how it changed from a Native

American homeland to a tourist destination. The museum has fascinating exhibits that explore the history of the island, including its connections to Hollywood and William Wrigley Jr., the chewing gum tycoon who was instrumental in Catalina's growth.

The museum regularly holds rotating exhibitions that showcase various parts of Catalina's culture and tradition in addition to the permanent exhibits. These exhibits offer educational opportunities for visitors of all ages, featuring anything from marine life to indigenous peoples.

These cultural institutions serve as important pit stops for anybody looking to gain a deeper understanding of the past and present of Catalina Island since they demonstrate the island's dedication to protecting its ecology and cultural legacy.

Heritage of Native Americans

With a history spanning millennia, Catalina Island has a strong Native American tradition.

The island's native inhabitants, particularly the Tongva, left a deep cultural mark that is still perceptible today.

You can take part in educational events and guided tours provided by groups like the Catalina Island Conservancy to learn more about this legacy. These trips offer insightful information about the Tongva people's traditional way of life, their interactions with the island's ecosystem, and their contributions to Catalina's cultural heritage.

Exploring historical items and learning about the customs and traditions of the island's original people is made possible by visiting archaeological sites like the Tongva Interpretive Center.

The island's history and the ongoing legacy of the Tongva people are highlighted through a variety of cultural events and festivals honoring Native American heritage. These encounters offer a strong link to Catalina's cultural origins and indigenous past.

Historical Events

Numerous cultural activities are held on Catalina Island, providing visitors with exceptional chances to experience the island's lively culture and sense of community.

The Avalon Ball, which takes participants back to the glitzy 1920s, is one noteworthy occasion. This lavish event, which takes place in the legendary Casino Ballroom, invites guests to dress to the nines in Gatsby-inspired fashion and dance the night away. It's a lovely blending of celebration, culture, and history.

Additionally, Catalina routinely organizes music festivals, live theater productions, and art fairs, giving both native and visiting artists a stage on which to display their talents. These activities develop a sense of community among island residents and tourists and a common love of the arts.

Catalina Island's cultural events perfectly encapsulate the island's distinct character and tight-knit community. They provide a wonderful opportunity to celebrate and interact with the local way of life.

Celebrations and Festivals

Throughout the year, Catalina Island comes to life with a variety of festivals and events, each of which offers a unique cultural experience.

The Catalina Island Film Festival, which presents independent films against the picturesque island backdrop, is one of the island's most well-known occasions. It is a celebration of filmmaking and frequently includes Q&A sessions with actors and directors.

The Catalina Island JazzTrax Festival, a musical extravaganza that draws jazz fans from all over the world, is another highlight. The main stage features world-class jazz performances in a unique setting at the island's famous Casino Ballroom.

With exciting parades and activities, the Buccaneer Days Festival honors the island's history of pirates. It's a fun event that transports guests to a time when pirates were active in the waters off Catalina.

These events provide tourists with wonderful opportunities to participate in the festivities and get a taste of Catalina's colorful culture. They also provide a distinctive cultural layer to the island's character.

Immersive Activities

Catalina Island provides a variety of immersive experiences that let guests engage deeply with the island's natural beauty and culture.

The Catalina Island Vineyards offers guided wine tastings for wine connoisseurs. These vineyards, which are situated in the picturesque island's interior, create distinctive wines, and excursions frequently include information on both the wine-making process and the history of the island.

Immersive spa retreats are available in Catalina for individuals wishing to unwind. The spas on the island combine luxury and peace, all while providing breathtaking ocean views.

Eco-tours are a wonderful opportunity to fully see Catalina's natural splendors. You may explore the island's interior on guided trips to see its rich vegetation and fauna. Exciting possibilities to enjoy the island's distinctive nature include zip-lining trips, underwater explorations, and wildlife encounters.

Visitors are able to discover the many elements of Catalina Island, from its natural wonders to its cultural riches, through these immersive experiences, developing lifelong memories and a deeper understanding of this extraordinary location.

Chapter 11: Nightlife and Entertainment

Pubs and bars

Catalina Island has a wonderful selection of pubs and taverns, each with its own distinctive personality. Here, you may choose between a calm atmosphere and a buzzing crowd. After a day of exploring, rest in one of the island's bars with a selection of artisan beers, local wines, or refreshing cocktails.

Visit a welcoming bar where you may mingle with both locals and tourists for a more relaxed experience. Bars on the water offer beautiful views of the Pacific Ocean if you're in the mood for some beach ambiance. Try the Buffalo Milk drink, a renowned Catalina creation, as soon as possible. It's a must-go place if you want to experience the island's nightlife and meet other travelers.

Live musical performance

Catalina Island offers a wide variety of live music events, making it a refuge for music lovers. The island has music for every taste, whether you prefer the soothing tones of an acoustic guitar or the energetic beats of a local band. Live music performances can be found in a variety of settings, from quaint clubs to beachfront bars.

Numerous great local musicians perform, resulting in a distinctive island ambiance that's ideal for a special night out. You might even run into special guests who enhance the musical enchantment on some nights. The live music on Catalina Island will make your evening memorable and harmonious, whether you're sipping a beverage or eating supper by the water.

Under the Stars Movie

The typical movie night is given a fantastic twist on Catalina Island. Imagine watching your favorite movies under a sky filled with stars. The island is where you can have this wonderful experience. You can often find friends and fellow visitors gathered on a beach or in a picturesque park for outdoor movie screenings.

A unique cinematic atmosphere is created by the soft ocean breeze, the whispering of the palm trees, and the twinkling stars overhead. The outdoor movie nights on Catalina Island are a great way to spend your evening in a laid-back and romantic atmosphere, whether it's a classic movie or a current release. Simply bring a blanket and some popcorn to enjoy the event outside.

Special Occasions

Not only is Catalina Island renowned for its natural beauty, but it also serves as a focal point for unique events that liven up your evenings with a dash of glitz and culture. The island holds numerous events all year long, including art exhibitions, wine tastings, cuisine festivals, and more. These events offer a special chance to interact with the locals and other tourists while enjoying the island's culture.

You can come across wine and dine events that let you enjoy delectable food and excellent wines in a picturesque location or art walks that feature the works of great local artists. The evening entertainment scene on Catalina Island is improved by these unique events, making it a prime location for anyone wanting a little class and culture on their night out.

Evening Activities

Your evenings will be memorable thanks to the variety of daring and distinctive nocturnal activities available on Catalina Island. Consider activities like night snorkeling if you want to spice up your nights a little. Discover the underwater realm when it is still dark and take in the ocean's enchanting bioluminescence.

Consider taking a moonlit stroll along the island's lovely beaches for a more relaxing experience. An atmosphere of peace and romance is produced by the softly lapping waves and the moon's mellow brightness.

Adventurers can also select guided night tours, which may involve excursions like zip-lining under the stars or night hikes through the island's untamed interior.

Catalina Island offers a variety of nocturnal activities to suit all interests, whether you enjoy the peace and quiet of the beach, the excitement of adventure, or a little bit of both.

Taking in the Starry Night

The chance to see the night sky is one of the most alluring features of Catalina Island's nightlife. The island provides outstanding stargazing conditions because there is less light pollution there. Simply relax on the beach or find a secluded area on a hilltop to take in the splendor of the constellations.

Join one of the island's astronomy tours for a more engaging experience. You will be introduced to the beauties of the night sky by knowledgeable guides who will share their insights on the stars, planets, and other celestial events. You may see faraway galaxies and nebulae up close with high-quality telescopes.

Catalina is the perfect place for those who value the wonder of the universe because of its quiet and clear nights, which offer a serene and breathtaking way to end your day on the island.

Chapter 12: Practical Information

Payments and Currency

The US dollar (USD) is accepted as payment in Catalina Island. In the center of Avalon, there are ATMs that you can use to get cash if necessary. The majority of establishments, including lodgings, eateries, and retail stores, take popular credit cards including Visa and MasterCard.

Nevertheless, it's a good idea to have extra cash on hand for smaller businesses, transit, or locations that might not accept cards. To prevent any problems with your credit or debit cards while on the island, it's also a good idea to let your bank know about your trip intentions. In general, Catalina Island accepts credit cards, however having some cash on hand can be useful.

The language used

Catalina Island's official language is English. English is commonly understood in the area, so communicating with people won't be a problem. English is the language of choice, whether you're looking for information, eating at a restaurant, or taking part in other activities.

Although you might come across bilingual workers in the tourism sector if you do happen to speak another language, it's always a good idea to have a few fundamental English expressions and phrases at the ready to improve your experience. English-speaking guests can easily feel at home on Catalina Island thanks to its kind atmosphere.

Connectivity and Wi-Fi

Catalina Island has some dependable connectivity possibilities, particularly in the hub city of Avalon. Customers may typically access free Wi-Fi at most hotels, eateries, and coffee shops. Public Wi-Fi hotspots are also accessible in well-known locations. However, be aware that due to the island's isolated location, you could occasionally experience internet problems, especially in more inner or quiet areas.

Consider getting a local SIM card with data packages if you need continual internet access as this can offer more dependable connectivity. It's a good idea to prepare for some offline activities and take advantage of the natural beauty and tranquility Catalina Island has to offer when visiting the island because you can encounter patchy signal coverage in some locations.

Packing Advice

It's important to pack appropriately for your trip to Catalina Island. Here are some suggestions for packing to make sure you have a wonderful time:

Pack comfortable, laid-back attire that is appropriate for the island's Mediterranean environment. The best textiles are those that breathe well. Don't forget your swimsuit since you'll probably want to cool off in the sea.

Footwear: If you intend to explore the island's hiking routes and picturesque places, you must wear comfortable walking shoes or sandals.

Sun protection: In order to be safe from the sun, you should wear sunscreen, sunglasses, and a wide-brimmed hat. On the island, the sun can be very powerful.

Hiking equipment is necessary if you intend to hike or explore the island's interior. This includes sturdy shoes, a daypack, and a reusable water bottle.

Layers: Because evenings can turn chilly, carry a lightweight jacket or sweater for comfort at night.

Reusable Water Bottles: Because the island emphasizes sustainability, think about bringing reusable water bottles to help reduce plastic waste.

Chargers and adapters: Don't forget to pack your gadgets' chargers as well as any required adapters for American power outlets.

Travel Documents: Make sure you have a copy of your identity, your passport, and your reservation information on hand.

You'll get the most out of your trip to Catalina Island if you follow these packing suggestions.

Island Protocol

To ensure a pleasant and courteous visit to Catalina Island, it's crucial to be aware of the island customs:

Environment Respect: Keep the island's natural beauty intact by abstaining from littering and according to the "Leave No Trace" guidelines. Keep to designated pathways to protect delicate habitats.

Enjoy watching the neighborhood wildlife from a safe distance without upsetting it. Animals shouldn't be fed because it can affect their natural behaviour and health.

Noise Levels: To preserve the quiet environment of the island, keep noise levels down, particularly in residential areas.

Water conservation is important because the island occasionally experiences water shortages. When you can, try to conserve water by taking shorter showers.

Tipping is traditional; in restaurants, it usually amounts to 15% to 20% of the tab. Verify the bill to see if a service fee has already been added.

Be Polite: Show respect for locals and other tourists. Simple courtesy goes a long way in keeping things cordial.

Respect the law and the rules: Follow all posted signs, instructions, and laws, especially those pertaining to beach activities, hiking, and the preservation of animals.

Respecting local customs not only assures a peaceful vacation but also helps the island promote sustainable tourism.

Sustainable travel

Sustainable tourism is highly valued on Catalina Island. During your visit, you may support this environmental project in the following ways:

Reduce, Reuse, Recycle: Bring reusable things like water bottles and shopping bags to reduce single-use plastic and participate in recycling programs.

Water conservation is important because the island occasionally experiences water shortages. Shorten your showers and adhere to any water-saving recommendations.

Hiking and Wildlife: To preserve the island's distinctive flora and animals, stick to the approved trails. Avoid feeding wildlife because it might interfere with their normal behavior.

Support Local Products: Buy locally produced and environmentally friendly things, such as mementos, to boost the island's economy and lessen the environmental impact of imported goods.

Practice responsible boating, which includes respecting marine life and properly disposing of debris, if you're exploring the seas around the island.

Education: Visit the Catalina Island Conservancy and other educational websites to learn more about the island's conservation initiatives.

You can contribute to the preservation of the ecological diversity and natural beauty that make Catalina Island a special and beloved vacation spot by embracing sustainable practices while you're there.

Important Contacts

It will be helpful to have a few important contacts available to you while you are on Catalina Island. Here are a few crucial contacts and phone numbers:

Services for Emergencies: Call 911 for quick assistance in an emergency. There are medical facilities and a hospital on the island.

Avalon Harbor Department: Contact the Avalon Harbor Department at [insert phone number] for information on boating and harbor-related issues.

Catalina Island Conservancy (CIC) Contact the Catalina Island Conservancy at [insert phone number] for details on hiking, nature, and conservation.
Contact the Catalina Island Visitor Center at [insert phone number] for basic information about the island, its attractions, and lodging options.

Transportation Services: Contact the appropriate companies or the Visitor Center for advice on available modes of transportation, such as ferries and tours.

Having these helpful people on hand can give you piece of mind and guarantee that you can get help or information if necessary when visiting Catalina Island.

Conclusion

Your Trip to Catalina Island

Your time on Catalina Island was a mesmerizing synthesis of the natural beauty and island charm. The sparkling seas and lush surroundings of this ideal paradise captured your senses the instant you stepped foot there. You experienced local fauna and stunning landscapes while hiking the island's rough trails, forging lifelong memories.

Your adventure gained a certain air of elegance thanks to Avalon's thriving culture, which includes its attractive stores and mouthwatering cuisine. You were thrilled by Catalina's many options, whether you were snorkeling in the clear waters, zip-lining across canyons, or just relaxing on the beach.

Living on an island provided a short-term respite from the rush and bustle of the mainland, and Catalina's serene air left an enduring impression.

As you depart, you take with you an indelible memory of the peace, excitement, and beauty of this magical island.

Islands in My Mind

Each island memory sparkles with the spirit of your Catalina journey, just like a valuable gem. These experiences will always hold a special place in your heart, whether it be the warm, sun-kissed beaches where you lazed around, the exciting snorkeling adventures that revealed a colorful underwater world, or the quiet evenings spent watching the sunset.

The memories are a tapestry of happiness and introspection. They include the joyous laughter shared with new friends, the hikes through pristine wilderness, and the peaceful moments of solitude on lonely coves. They remind you of the beauty that exists in the world by taking you back to a tranquil setting full of natural wonder.

These island memories serve as a reminder of the value of exploration and the relevance of cherishing life's most beautiful moments when you think back on them. Every memory serves as a monument to Catalina's charm and the beauty of the unexplored universe.

Going back to the Mainland

The moment you leave Catalina Island is bittersweet. Your farewell to the serene paradise you've grown to love is the boat voyage back to the mainland. You can't help but experience a sense of longing as you see the island's outline vanish on the horizon.

A range of emotions are brought with the return to the mainland. On the one hand, you're eager to tell your friends and family about your adventures. While you eagerly anticipate returning home, you also have to say goodbye to the tranquil island lifestyle that has shaped who you are.

You think back on the amazing adventure you had and the memories you made as you get closer to the mainland. It serves as a reminder that even after you depart from our island paradise, Catalina's magic will live on in your memories as a treasured chapter of your life's story.

Share Your Experience

The experience of traveling to Catalina Island with friends and family is enjoyable. You entertain them with tales of the island's distinctive charm, fascinating adventures, and turquoise oceans. They are spellbound by the pictures you paint with your storytelling, and they hang on your every word.

As you narrate the experiences of snorkeling with a variety of fish, discovering undiscovered coves, and enjoying regional food, your images and videos bring the island's beauty to life. Others are encouraged to think of going on their own island adventures by your contagious excitement.

Sharing your experience allows you to inspire people to go on their own journeys rather than just reliving your own. By inspiring others to travel and have their own life-changing experiences, your storytelling ignites their own wanderlust.

Your trip doesn't end with you; it keeps inspiring others and igniting their curiosity and sense of adventure.

Goodbye, Catalina

It's like saying goodbye to a close friend when you say goodbye to Catalina Island. Your heart has been permanently changed by the island's stunning natural surroundings, peaceful atmosphere, and kind friendliness of its residents. You can't help but turn around as you get aboard the boat and take in the breathtaking views of the island disappearing into the distance.

The moments you've created while here will be treasured always. Your memory will forever be seared by the breathtaking sunsets, secret beaches, and peaceful moments. The allure of

Catalina has a way of becoming woven into your very being.

Even if you are leaving the island, you carry with you the serenity, the spirit of adventure, and the profound respect for nature's beauty. We bid Catalina farewell, but it won't be a permanent parting. Returning to the island will always be a source of inspiration and pleasure.

Your Upcoming Journey

While leaving Catalina Island could make you feel a little melancholy, it also makes you eager for your upcoming journey. Your attention automatically shifts to the future when you get back on shore. You're prepared to embark on the next phase of your journey as there are many places in the world that are just waiting to be discovered.

Maybe you're thinking about traveling to another ideal location since you want to find new things and make new memories. Or perhaps you've already begun making plans to visit Catalina again, confident that this idyllic island will always be on your list of places to visit.

Catalina has given you a desire to travel and a thirst for knowledge, which will serve you well on whatever trip you decide to go on. The world is your oyster, and with every journey you take, you add a new, bright pearl to your collection of encounters. So, while you say goodbye to Catalina, you also throw open the door to all the adventures that are still to come.

We appreciate your visit

We sincerely appreciate you choosing Catalina Island as your travel location. Not only has your visit benefited our neighborhood, but it has also warmed and gratefully filled our hearts.

We hope your stay was memorable, from discovering our natural landscapes to getting to know our island's distinctive culture. We appreciate the chance to share our little piece of paradise with you and how your presence has added to the rich tapestry of our neighborhood.

We hope that as you depart, a bit of Catalina will stay with you as a memento of the peaceful moments, exhilarating experiences, and real hospitality you encountered. You are always welcome to visit our island, and we look forward to sharing more special moments with you in the future.

I want to thank you once more for coming. We are forever changed by your journey, and we hope that you continue to feel more and more a part of Catalina Island every day.

Recognition and Credits

Every excellent event has a number of people and efforts to thank behind it. We want to thank everyone who helped make your trip to Catalina Island possible.

We would like to express our gratitude to the residents for creating the special ambiance you have experienced and for their warm welcome and commitment to maintaining the island's natural beauty. The establishments, tour operators, and employees who put in such much effort to make your visit unforgettable deserve our appreciation.

We also like to thank the environmentalists and conservationists for their work in preserving Catalina's sensitive ecosystem and letting you enjoy its untainted beauty.

Finally, we want to express our gratitude to you, the guest, for picking Catalina and for traveling sensibly. Your sensitivity to the island's ecology and culture assures that subsequent generations will be able to appreciate this wonderful location.

The magic of Catalina Island is a result of these unified efforts and acknowledgments, I might say. We wish you well as you continue to travel the globe and make cherished memories while promoting ethical and sustainable tourism.